With love to our little angel, Zach
~ Mimi

THE WISE ANIMAL HANDBOOK

Kate B. Jerome

ARCADIA KIDS

Attempt new skills from time to time.

Just **try** to think them **through.**

And if you find you're left behind...

...then change your point of view.

Try not to think of just yourself.

Invent new ways to share.

Stay close to friends whom you can trust.

But always be aware.

Avoid the tattle in the tale.

Insist that **truth** is **best.**

Embrace with pride the strengths you have.

Demand
to be
impressed.

Enjoy the peace that nature brings.

Ignore what's just for show.

Join **forces** when the road gets **rough**.

Admit
when you
don't know.

Remember family is the best.

Despite the ups and downs.

Don't **hide** from things that you must **face.**

Make joyful laughing sounds.

Eat **healthy** food to **grow** up **strong.**

Be patient with your friends.

Try not to take a stubborn stand.

Be
quick
to make
amends.

Excuse yourself when **manners** slip.

Be **helpful** every **day.**

Keep trying even when it's hard.

But don't forget to play!

And
sing

...and dance each day!

Written by Kate B. Jerome
Design and Production: Lumina Datamatics, Inc.
Coloring Illustrations: Tom Pounders
Research: Eric Nyquist

Cover Images: See back cover

Interior Images: 002 Anetapics/Shutterstock.com; 003 George Green/Shutterstock.com; 004 Sergey Uryadnikov/Shutterstock.com; 005 Gnomeandi/Shutterstock.com; 006 Bruce MacQueen/Shutterstock.com; 007 Henk Bentlage/Shutterstock.com; 008 M.M./Shutterstock.com; 009 Mikael Damkier/Shutterstock.com; 010 Brendan van Son/Shutterstock.com; 011 Michael Pettigrew/Shutterstock.com; 012 StevenRussellSmithPhotos/Shutterstock.com; 013 Pakhnyushchy/Shutterstock.com; 014 Patjo/Shutterstock.com; 015 Quinn Martin/Shutterstock.com; 016 Lincoln Rogers/Shutterstock.com; 017 Dirk Ercken/Shutterstock.com; 018 Karel Gallas/Shutterstock.com; 019 Orangecrush/Shutterstock.com; 020 Guenter-foto/Shutterstock.com; 021 Janecat/Shutterstock.com; 022 Shironina/Shutterstock.com; 023 Annette Shaff/Shutterstock.com; 024 Vitaly Titov/Shutterstock.com; 025 Rohappy/Shutterstock.com; 026 MattiaATH/Shutterstock.com; 027 Otsphoto/Shutterstock.com; 028 FikMik/Shutterstock.com; 029 Four Oaks/Shutterstock.com; 030 Ekaterina Kolomeets/Shutterstock.com; 031 Hugh Lansdown/Shutterstock.com.

Published by Arcadia Kids, a division of Arcadia Publishing and
The History Press, Charleston, SC

For all general information contact Arcadia Publishing at:
Telephone: 843-853-2070
Email: sales@arcadiapublishing.com

For Customer Service and Orders:
Toll Free: 1-888-313-2665
Visit us on the Internet at www.arcadiapublishing.com

Library of Congress Cataloging-in-Publication data is on file with the publisher.

Printed in China

New York State Animal

Beaver

Read Together

The beaver was named the state animal in 1975. This critter has waterproof fur and a flat tail to help it build dams.

New York State **Bird**

Eastern Bluebird

Read Together

The eastern bluebird was name the state bird in 1970. The robin was first suggested as the state bird, but the bluebird finally won top spot!

New York State Reptile

Snapping Turtle

Read Together

The snapping turtle was named the state reptile in 2006. They live in lakes, ponds, rivers, and streams throughout New York. But they have a very nasty bite, so be sure to stay away!

New York State Freshwater Fish

Brook Trout

© Kate B. Jerome 2017

Read Together

The brook trout was named the state's freshwater fish in 1975. (The striped bass is the state's saltwater fish.)